N4 KANJI FOR BEGINNERS

All rights reserved. 2025
No part of this publication may be reproduced, stored in a retrieval system, or transmitted in any form or by any means, whether electronic, mechanical, photocopying, recording, or by any other process, without prior authorization.

Introduction to the 168 Most Important Kanji for N4

Kanji is a fundamental part of the Japanese language, and mastering it is essential for improving reading and writing skills. This list contains the 168 most important kanji for the N4 level, carefully selected to include the most frequently used characters in daily communication, media, and basic texts.

While the full N4 kanji list typically includes around 300 characters, these 168 kanji represent the core symbols that appear most often in texts and conversations at this level. Learning these will significantly enhance your ability to understand and use Japanese in practical situations.

- ### How to Effectively Learn These 168 Kanji?

Focus on radicals – Understanding the smaller components of kanji makes memorization easier.

Practice writing – Writing kanji by hand reinforces recognition and recall.

Learn in context – Study kanji within sentences to grasp their meaning more naturally.

Use flashcards – Apps like Anki or Quizlet help reinforce learning through spaced repetition (SRS).

Read and recognize – Exposure to kanji in real texts helps build fluency.

Mastering these 168 essential kanji will give you a strong foundation for the N4 level and prepare you for more advanced Japanese study. Keep practicing and enjoy your progress!

N4 KANJI LIST

不 (fu)	世 (sei)	主 (shu)	乗 (jou)	事 (ji)	京 (kyou)
仕 (shi)	代 (dai)	以 (i)	低 (tei)	住 (juu)	体 (tai)
作 (saku)	使 (shi)	便 (ben)	借 (shaku)	働 (dou)	元 (gen)
兄 (kyou)	光 (kou)	写 (sha)	冬 (tou)	切 (setsu)	別 (betsu)
力 (ryoku)	勉 (ben)	動 (dou)	区 (ku)	医 (i)	去 (kyo)
台 (dai)	合 (gou)	同 (dou)	味 (mi)	品 (hin)	員 (in)
問 (mon)	回 (kai)	図 (zu)	地 (chi)	堂 (dou)	場 (jou)
声 (sei)	売 (bai)	夏 (ka)	夕 (seki)	夜 (ya)	太 (tai)
好 (kou)	妹 (mai)	姉 (shi)	始 (shi)	字 (ji)	室 (shitsu)
家 (ka)	寒 (kan)	屋 (oku)	工 (kou)	市 (shi)	帰 (ki)
広 (kou)	度 (do)	建 (ken)	引 (in)	弟 (dai)	弱 (jaku)
強 (kyou)	待 (tai)	心 (shin)	思 (shi)	急 (kyuu)	悪 (aku)
意 (i)	所 (sho)	持 (ji)	教 (kyou)	文 (bun)	料 (ryou)
重 (juu)	野 (ya)	銀 (gin)	門 (mon)	開 (kai)	院 (in)

N4 KANJI LIST

方 (hou)	旅 (ryo)	族 (zoku)	早 (sou)	明 (myou)	映 (ei)
春 (shun)	昼 (chuu)	暑 (sho)	暗 (an)	曜 (you)	有 (yuu)
服 (fuku)	朝 (chou)	村 (son)	林 (rin)	森 (shin)	業 (gyou)
楽 (gaku)	歌 (ka)	止 (shi)	正 (sei)	歩 (ho)	死 (shi)
民 (min)	池 (chi)	注 (chuu)	洋 (you)	洗 (sen)	海 (kai)
漢 (kan)	牛 (gyuu)	物 (butsu)	特 (toku)	犬 (ken)	理 (ri)
産 (san)	用 (you)	田 (den)	町 (chou)	画 (ga)	界 (kai)
病 (byou)	発 (hatsu)	県 (ken)	真 (shin)	着 (chaku)	知 (chi)
短 (tan)	研 (ken)	私 (shi)	秋 (shuu)	究 (kyuu)	答 (tou)
紙 (shi)	終 (shuu)	習 (shuu)	考 (kou)	者 (sha)	肉 (niku)
自 (ji)	色 (shiki)	英 (ei)	茶 (cha)	菜 (sai)	薬 (yaku)
親 (shin)	計 (kei)	試 (shi)	説 (setsu)	貸 (tai)	質 (shitsu)
赤 (seki)	走 (sou)	起 (ki)	転 (ten)	軽 (kei)	近 (kin)
送 (sou)	通 (tsuu)	進 (shin)	運 (un)	遠 (en)	都 (to)

KANJI PRACTICE WORKSHEET

不	Negative, non- フ fun, ブ bu

Compounds:

不足
ふそく fusoku
insufficiency, shortage

不安
ふあん fuan
anxiety, uneasiness

不当
ふとう futou
injustice, unfair

不全
ふぜん fuzen
partial, incomplete

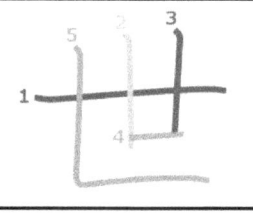

世	World, public, society セ se, セイ sei よ yo

Compounds:

世界
せかい sekai
world, society

世代
せだい sedai
generation, age

世話
せわ sewa
looking after, help

KANJI PRACTICE WORKSHEET

主	Main, principle シュ shu おも omo
Compounds: 主 おも omo main, principal, important 主人 しゅじん shujin master, landlord, husband, employer 主食 しゅしょく shushoku staple food	

乗	To ride, to get on ジョウ jou の(る) noru
Compounds: 乗員 じょういん jouin crew 乗り場 のりば noriba place for boarding vehicles 乗り物 のりもの norimono vehicle	

KANJI PRACTICE WORKSHEET

事	Matter, thing ジ ji こと koto

Compounds:

仕事
しごと shigoto
work, occupation

火事
かじ kaji
fire

食事
しょくじ shokuji
meal

京	Capital キョウ kyou, ケイ kei

Compounds:

東京
とうきょう
Tokyo - Capital of Japan

京子
きょうこ
kyoko

京都
きょうと
kyoto

KANJI PRACTICE WORKSHEET

仕	Attend, do シ shi

Compounds:

仕事
　しごと shigoto
　work, occupation

仕事場
　しごとば shigotoba
　place where one works

仕上げる
　しあげる
　ahiawaseru
　to finish up, to complete

代	Age, generation, substitute ダイ dai か（わる） ka(waru)

Compounds:

代わる
　かわる kawaru
　to take the place of

時代
　じだい jidai
　period, era

世代
　せだい sedai
　generation, age

KANJI PRACTICE WORKSHEET

以	By means of イ i

Compounds:

以下
いか ika
less than, below, under

以内
いない inai
within, inside of

以外
いがい igai
with the exception of

低	Short, humble テイ tei ひく(い) hikui

Compounds:

低い
ひくい
short, low, humble

低音
ていおん
low tone, bass

低下
ていか
fall, decline

KANJI PRACTICE WORKSHEET

住	Live, reside ジュウ　juu す(む)sumu

Compounds:

住む
すむ sumu
　to reside, to live in

住所
　じゅうしょ juusho
　address (eg house), residence

安住
　あんじゅう anjuu
　living peaceably

体	Object, body タイ　tai からだ　　　karada

Compounds:

本体
　ほんたい hontai
　substance, real form

死体
　したい shitai
　corpse

人体
　じんたい jintai
　human body

KANJI PRACTICE WORKSHEET

以

By means of

イ i

Compounds:

以下
いか ika
less than, below, under

以内
いない inai
within, inside of

以外
いがい igai
with the exception of

低

Short, humble

テイ tei
ひく(い) hikui

Compounds:

低い
ひくい
short, low, humble

低音
ていおん
low tone, bass

低下
ていか
fall, decline

KANJI PRACTICE WORKSHEET

住	Live, reside ジュウ juu す (む)sumu

Compounds:

住む
すむ sumu
to reside, to live in

住所
じゅうしょ juusho
address (eg house), residence

安住
あんじゅう anjuu
living peaceably

体	Object, body タイ tai からだ　　karada

Compounds:

本体
ほんたい hontai
substance, real form

死体
したい shitai
corpse

人体
じんたい jintai
human body

KANJI PRACTICE WORKSHEET

作	Make, create サク　saku つく(る)　tsuku(ru)

Compounds:

作る
つくる tsukuru
to make, to create

工作
こうさく kousaku
work, handicraft

作り話
つくりはなし
tsukurihanashi
fiction, made-up story, myth

使	To use シ　shi つか(う)　tsuka(u)

Compounds:

使い方
つかいかた
tsukaikata
way to use something

天使
てんし tenshi
angel

使者
ししゃ shisha
messenger

KANJI PRACTICE WORKSHEET

便	Convenience, post ベン ben ビン bin たよ(り) tayori

Compounds:

便
びん bin
mail, post

不便
ふべん fuben
inconvenience

小便
しょうべん
shouben
urine

借	Borrow, rent シャク shaku か(りる) kariru

Compounds:

借りる
かりる kariru
to borrow

借金
しゃっきん shakkin
debt, loan, liabilities

借り物
かりもの karimono
borrowed thing

KANJI PRACTICE WORKSHEET

働	Work ドウ dou はたら（く）hataraku

Compounds:

働く
はたらく hataraku
to work, to labour

働き者
はたらきもの
hatarakimono
hardworker, hard working person

働き口
はたらきぐち
hatarakiguchi
position, opening

元	Beginning, origin ガン gan, ゲン gen もと moto

Compounds:

元気
げんき genki
health, spirit

耳元
みみもと
mimimoto
close to the ear

地元
じもと jimoto
local

KANJI PRACTICE WORKSHEET

兄	Elder brother キョウ kyou あに ani
Compounds: お兄さん おにいさん oniisan (someone else's) elder brother 兄 あに ani (your own) elder brother 父兄 ふけい fukei guardians	(practice grid)

光	Light, ray コウ kou ひかり hikari, ひか(る) hikaru
Compounds: 電光 でんこう denkou lightning 月光 げっこう gekkou moonlight 日光 にっこう nikkou sunlight	(practice grid)

KANJI PRACTICE WORKSHEET

働	Work ドウ dou はたら（く）hataraku
Compounds: 働く はたらく hataraku to work, to labour 働き者 はたらきもの hatarakimono hardworker, hard working person 働き口 はたらきぐち hatarakiguchi position, opening	(practice grid)

元	Beginning, origin ガン gan, ゲン gen もと moto
Compounds: 元気 げんき genki health, spirit 耳元 みみもと mimimoto close to the ear 地元 じもと jimoto local	(practice grid)

KANJI PRACTICE WORKSHEET

兄

Elder brother

キョウ kyou
あに ani

Compounds:

お兄さん
おにいさん oniisan
(someone else's) elder brother

兄
あに ani
(your own) elder brother

父兄
ふけい fukei
guardians

光

Light, ray

コウ kou
ひかり hikari, ひか(る) hikaru

Compounds:

電光
でんこう denkou
lightning

月光
げっこう gekkou
moonlight

日光
にっこう nikkou
sunlight

KANJI PRACTICE WORKSHEET

写

Copy, describe

シャ sha
うつ(す) utsusu

Compounds:

写す
うつす utsusu
to copy, to duplicate

写真
しゃしん shashin
photograph

写真屋
しゃしんや
shashinya
photo studio

冬

Winter

トウ tou
ふゆ fuyu

Compounds:

冬場
ふゆば fuyuba
winter season

冬物
ふゆもの fuyumono
winter clothing

冬日
ふゆび fuyubi
the winter sun

KANJI PRACTICE WORKSHEET

切	Cut, be sharp セツ setsu き (る) kiru

Compounds:

切る
きる kiru
to cut, to chop

大切
たいせつ taisetsu
important, valuable

親切
しんせつ shinsetsu
kind

別	Separate, extra ベツ betsu わか(れる) wakareru

Compounds:

別
べつ betsu
another, particular

別に
べつに betsuni
(not) particularly, nothing

特別
とくべつ tokubetsu
special

KANJI PRACTICE WORKSHEET

力	Power, strength リキ riki, リョク　　ryoku ちから chikara
Compounds: 電力 　でんりょく 　denryoku 　electric power 全力 　ぜんりょく 　zenryoku 　all one's power 力持ち 　ちからもち 　chikaramochi 　muscle man	(practice grid with traced 力 characters)

勉	Exertion ベン ben
Compounds: 勉強 　べんきょう 　benkyou 　study, diligence 勉学 　べんがく bengaku 　study, pursuit of 　knowledge 不勉強 　ふべんきょう 　fubenkyou 　idleness	(practice grid with traced 勉 characters)

KANJI PRACTICE WORKSHEET

動

Move, change

うごく　　ugoku
どう dou

Compounds:

動く
うごく ugoku
to move

動物
どうぶつ doubutsu
animal

自動
じどう jidou
automatic

区

Section, zone

く ku

Compounds:

区
く ku
ward, district, section

区別
くべつ kubetsu
distinction, differentiation, classification

区間
くかん kukan
section

KANJI PRACTICE WORKSHEET

医

Doctor, medicine

イ i

Compounds:

医者
いしゃ isha
doctor (medical)

医学
いがく igaku
medical science

医院
いいん iin
doctor's office

去

Leave, past

キョ kyo
さ(る) saru

Compounds:

去年
きょねん kyonen
last year

去来
きょらい kyorai
coming and going

死去
しきょ shikyo
death

KANJI PRACTICE WORKSHEET

台	Stand, pedestal ダイ dai タイ tai

Compounds:

台
だい dai
stand, rack

台風
たいふう taifuu
typhoon

台所
だいどころ
daidokoro
kitchen

合	Fit, suit カッ, ガッ, ゴウ　ka', ga', gou あ (う) au

Compounds:

合う
あう au
to fit, to suit, to match

試合
しあい shiai
match, tournament

似合う
にあう niau
to suit

KANJI PRACTICE WORKSHEET

同	Same, equal ドウ dou おな(じ) onaji

Compounds:

同じ
おなじ onaji
same, similar

同時
どうじ douji
simultaneously, concurrent, same time

同意
どうい doui
agreement

味	Flavour, taste ミ mi あじ aji

Compounds:

味
あじ aji
taste, flavour

意味
いみ imi
meaning, significance

地味
じみ jimi
plain, simple

KANJI PRACTICE WORKSHEET

品

Goods, refinement

ヒン hin
しな shina

Compounds:

品物
 しなもの
 shinamono
 goods, article, thing

部品
 ぶひん buhin
 parts, accessories

品名
 ひんめい hinmei
 product name

員

Employee, member

イン in

Compounds:

店員
 てんいん tenin
 shop assistant, employee

工員
 こういん kouin
 factory worker

楽員
 がくいん gakuin
 band member

KANJI PRACTICE WORKSHEET

問	Question, problem モン mon とん ton, と(う) tou

Compounds:

問題
　もんだい mondai
　problem, question

不問
　ふもん fumon
　ignorance

自問
　じもん jimon
　asking oneself

回	Round, -times カイ kai まわ(る) mawaru

Compounds:

回る
　まわる mawaru
　to turn, to revolve,
　to visit several places

何回
　なんかい nankai
　how many times?

乗り回す
　のりまわす
　norimawasu
　to ride/drive around

KANJI PRACTICE WORKSHEET

図

Map, plan

ズ zu, ト to
はか(る) hakaru

Compounds:

図
ず zu
drawing, picture, illustration

地図
ちず chizu
map

意図
いと ito
intention, aim, design

地

Ground, earth

ジ ji, チ chi

Compounds:

地
ち chi
earth

地下
ちか chika
basement, underground

地図
ちず chizu
map

KANJI PRACTICE WORKSHEET

堂	Hall, public chamber ドウ dou

Compounds:

堂
どう dou
 temple, shrin, hall

会堂
かいどう kaidou
 church, chapel

本堂
ほんどう hondou
 main temple building

場	location, place ジョウ jou ば ba

Compounds:

場
ば ba
 place

立場
たちば tachiba
 standpoint, position, situation

工場
こうじょう koujou
 factory, plant, mill

広場
ひろば hiroba
 plaza

KANJI PRACTICE WORKSHEET

声	Voice, sound セイ sei こえ koe

Compounds:

声
こえ koe
voice

小声
こごえ kogoe
soft voice, whisper

話し声
はなしごえ
hanashigoe
speaking voice

売	Sell バイ bai う(る) u(ru)

Compounds:

売る
うる uru
to sell

発売
はつばい hatsubai
sale

売り場
うりば uriba
place where things
are sold

KANJI PRACTICE WORKSHEET

夏	Summer カ ka なつ natsu

Compounds:

夏
なつ natsu
summer

夏休み
なつやすみ
natsuyasumi
summer holiday

夏時間
なつじかん
natsujikan
summer time

夕	Evening セキ seki ゆう yuu

Compounds:

夕べ
ゆうべ yuube
evening

七夕
たなばた tanabata
Star Festival

夕方
ゆうがた yuugata
evening

KANJI PRACTICE WORKSHEET

夜	Evening, night ヤ ya よる yoru

Compounds:

夜
 よる yoru
 evening

今夜
 こんや konya
 tonight, this evening

夜学
 やがく yagaku
 night school

太	Thick, plump タ ta, タイ tai ふと(い) futo(i), ふと(る) futo(ru)

Compounds:

太い
 ふとい futoi
 thick

太る
 ふとる futoru
 to be on the heavy side

太字
 ふとじ futoji
 bold type

KANJI PRACTICE WORKSHEET

好	Pleasing, like コウ kou す (き)

Compounds:

好き
　すき suki
　to like

好意
　こうい koui
　good will, favour

好都合
　こうつごう
　koutsugou
　convenient,
　favourable

妹	Younger sister マイ mai いもうと　imouto

Compounds:

妹
　いもうと imouto
　younger sister

姉妹
　しまい shimai
　sisters

妹川
　いもがわ imogawa
　Imogawa
　(location)

KANJI PRACTICE WORKSHEET

姉	Elder sister シ shi あね ane

Compounds:

姉
 あね ane
 (your own) older sister

姉妹
 しまい shimai
 sisters

お姉さん
 おねえさん
 oneesan
 (someone elses) older sister

始	Begin, commence シ shi はじ(める) haji(meru)

Compounds:

始める
 はじめる hajimeru
 to start, to begin

年始
 ねんし nenshi
 new year

始業
 しぎょう shigyou
 start work

KANJI PRACTICE WORKSHEET

字	Character, letter ジ ji

Compounds:

字
じ ji
character, letter, word

漢字
かんじ kanji
kanji, chinese characters

赤字
あかじ akaji
deficit

室	Room シツ shitsu

Compounds:

室
しつ shitsu
room

教室
きょうしつ
kyoushitsu
classroom

室内
しつない shitsunai
in the room

KANJI PRACTICE WORKSHEET

家	House, home カ ka, ケ ke いえ ie

Compounds:

家
いえ ie
house, one's home

家族
かぞく kazoku
family

画家
がか gaka
painter

寒	Cold カン kan さむ(い) samu(i)

Compounds:

寒い
さむい samui
cold (weather)

寒がり
さむがり samugari
senstive to cold

悪寒
おかん okan
chill, shakes

KANJI PRACTICE WORKSHEET

屋	House, roof オク oku や ya

Compounds:

屋上
おくじょう okujou
rooftop

料理屋
りょうりや
ryouriya
restaurant

屋外
おくがい okugai
outdoors

屋内
おくない okunai
indoors

工	Craft, construction コウ kou

Compounds:

工場
こうじょう koujou
factory, workshop

人工
じんこう jinkou
artificial, man-made

工学
こうがく kougaku
engineering

KANJI PRACTICE WORKSHEET

市	City, town シ shi いち ichi

Compounds:

市
  し shi
  city, town

市民
  しみん shimin
  citizen, townspeople

市内
  しない shinai
  within a city

帰	Return キ ki かえ(る) kae(ru)

Compounds:

帰る
  かえる kaeru
  to return, to go back, to go home

お帰り
  おかえり okaeri
  return, welcome

持ち帰り
  もちかえり mochikaeri
  takeout

KANJI PRACTICE WORKSHEET

広	Wide, spacious コウ kou ひろ(い) hiro(i)					
Compounds: 広い ひろい hiroi spacious, wide 広める ひろめる hiromeru to broaden, to propogate 広場 ひろば hiroba plaza	広	広	広	広	広	広
	広	広	広	広	広	広
	広	広	広	広	広	広
	広	広	広	広	広	広
	広	広	広	広	広	広
	広	広	広	広	広	広
	広	広	広	広	広	広
	広	広	広	広	広	広

度	Degree, occurrence ド do					
Compounds: 何度 なんど nando how many times? how often? 度 ど do counter for occurrences 強度 きょうど kyoudo strength	度	度	度	度	度	度
	度	度	度	度	度	度
	度	度	度	度	度	度
	度	度	度	度	度	度
	度	度	度	度	度	度
	度	度	度	度	度	度
	度	度	度	度	度	度
	度	度	度	度	度	度

KANJI PRACTICE WORKSHEET

	Build ケン ken た(てる) ta(teru)
Compounds: 建物 たてもの tatemono building 建てる たてる tateru to build, to construct 建前 たてまえ tatemae official stance	(practice grid)

	Pull イン in ひ(く) hi(ku)
Compounds: 引く ひく hiku to pull 引き出し ひきだし hikidashi drawer 引用 いによう iniyou quotation	(practice grid)

KANJI PRACTICE WORKSHEET

弟	Younger brother ダイ　dai, テイ　tei, デ　de おとうと　　otouto

Compounds:

弟
おとうと otouto
younger brother

弟妹
ていまい teimai
younger brother and sister

兄弟
きょうだい kyoudai
siblings

弱	Weak ジャク　jaku よわ(い) yowa(i)

Compounds:

弱い
よわい yowai
weak, frail, delicate

弱者
じゃくしゃ jakusha
the weak

弱み
よわみ yowami
weakness

弱虫
よわむし
yowamushi
weakling, coward

KANJI PRACTICE WORKSHEET

強	Strong キョウ　kyou つよ(い)　tsuyo(i)

Compounds:

強い
つよい tsuyoi
strong

勉強
べんきょう
benkyou
study, diligence

強気
つよき tsuyoki
firm, strong

待	Wait タイ tai ま (つ) ma(tsu)

Compounds:

待つ
まつ matsu
to wait

待合
まちあい machiai
meeting place

待ち合わせ
まちあわせ
machiawase
appointment

KANJI PRACTICE WORKSHEET

心

Heart, spirit, mind

シン shin
こころ kokoro

Compounds:

心
こころ kokoro
heart, mind, spirit

安心
あんしん anshin
relief, peace of mind

心中
しんちゅう
shinchuu
in one's heart

思

Think

シ shi
おも(う) omo(u)

Compounds:

思う
おもう omou
to think, to feel

思い
おもい omoi
thought

思い上がる
おもいあがる
omoiagaru
to be conceited

KANJI PRACTICE WORKSHEET

急	Hurry, sudden キュウ kyuu いそ(ぐ) iso(gu)

Compounds:

急
 きゅう kyuu
 urgent, sudden, steep

急ぐ
 いそぐ isogu
 to hurry, to rush

急行
 きゅうこう
 kyuukou
 express train

悪	Bad, wrong, evil アク aku わる(い) waru(i)

Compounds:

悪い
 わるい warui
 bad, inferior

最悪
 さいあく saiaku
 the worst

悪質
 あくしつ akushitsu
 bad quality

KANJI PRACTICE WORKSHEET

意	Idea, thought, mind イ i

Compounds:

意味
いみ imi
meaning

意見
いけん iken
opinion, view

注意
ちゅうい chuui
caution

所	Place ショ sho ところ tokoro

Compounds:

所
ところ tokoro
place

場所
ばしょ basho
place, location

住所
じゅうしょ juusho
address

KANJI PRACTICE WORKSHEET

持	Hold, have ジ ji も (つ) mo(tsu)					
Compounds: 持つ もつ motsu to have, to hold, to carry 気持ち きもち kimochi feeling, sensation, mood 持ち出す もちだす mochidasu to take out						

教	Teach キョウ kyou おし(える) oshi(eru)					
Compounds: 教える おしえる oshieru to teach, to inform 教え おしえ oshie teaching, lesson 教師 きょうし kyoushi Teacher						

KANJI PRACTICE WORKSHEET

文

モン mon
ブン bun
ふみ fumi

Sentence

Compounds:

文 ぶん bun
sentence

文学 ぶんがく bungaku
literature

文書 ぶんしょ bunsho
document

料

リョウ ryou

Fee, materials

Compounds:

料理 りょうり ryouri
cooking, cuisine

料金 りょうきん ryoukin
fee, charge

試料 しりょう shiryou
sample

KANJI PRACTICE WORKSHEET

重	Heavy, pile up チョウ chou ジュウ juu おも(い) omo(i)

Compounds:

重い
おもい omoi
heavy

重大
じゅうだい juudai
serious, important, grave

体重
たいじゅう taijuu
one's body weight

野	Plain, field ヤ ya の no

Compounds:

野菜
やさい yasai
vegetable

野鳥
やちょう yachou
(wild) bird

野外
やがい yagai
suburbs

KANJI PRACTICE WORKSHEET

銀	Silver ギン gin

Compounds:

銀行
ぎんこう ginkou
bank

銀色
ぎんいろ giniro
silver

水銀
すいぎん suigin
mercury

門	Gates モン mon

Compounds:

門
もん mon
gate

門下
もんか monka
one's pupil or follower

入門
にゅうもん nyuumon
primer

KANJI PRACTICE WORKSHEET

開

Open

カイ kai
あ (く) a(ku)

Compounds:

開く
あく aku
To open

開店
かいてん kaiten
Open (store)

開閉
かいへい kaihei
switch

院

Institution

イン in

Compounds:

病院
びょういん byouin
hospital

学院
がくいん gakuin
institute, academy

大学院
だいがくいん
daigakuin
graduate school

KANJI PRACTICE WORKSHEET

方	Direction, person ホウ hou かた kata

Compounds:

方
かた kata
Person

考え方
かんがえかた
kangaekata
way of thinking

見方
みかた mikata
viewpoint

旅	Trip, travel リョ ryo たび tabi

Compounds:

旅
たび tabi
travel, trip, journey

旅行
りょこう ryokou
travel, trip

旅館
りょかん ryokan
Japanese-style hotel

KANJI PRACTICE WORKSHEET

族

Family, tribe

ゾク zoku

Compounds:

家族
かぞく kazoku
family, members of family

水族館
すいぞくかん
suizokukan
aquarium

王族
おうぞく ouzoku
royalty

早

Early, fast

ソウ sou
はや(い) haya(i)

Compounds:

早い
はやい hayai
early

早口
はやくち hayakuchi
fast talking

早起き
はやおき hayaoki
early rising

KANJI PRACTICE WORKSHEET

明	Light, bright ミョウ myou メイ mei あか(るい) aka(rui)

Compounds:

明るい
あかるい akarui
bright, cheerful

説明
せつめい setsumei
explanation

不明
ふめい fumei
unknown

映	Reflect, projection エイ ei うつ(る) utsu(ru)

Compounds:

映画
えいが eiga
movie, film

映る
うつる utsuru
to be reflected, to harmonize with

映画館
えいがかん eigakan
movie theatre, cinema

KANJI PRACTICE WORKSHEET

春	Spring はる haru
Compounds: 春 はる haru spring	(practice grid)

昼	Daytime, noon チュウ chuu ひる hiru
Compounds: 昼食 ちゅうしょく chuushoku lunch 昼休み ひるやすみ Hiruyasumi Afternoon rest 昼ご飯 ひるごはん hirugohan Lunch break	(practice grid)

KANJI PRACTICE WORKSHEET

暑	Hot あつ(い) atsu(i)					
Compounds: 暑い あつい atsui hot 暑さ あつさ atsusa heat 暑中 しょちゅう shochuu mid-summer						

暗	Darkness, dark くら(い) kura(i)					
Compounds: 暗い くらい kurai dark, gloomy 真っ暗 まっくら makkura total darkness, pitch dark 暗に あんに anni implicitly						

KANJI PRACTICE WORKSHEET

曜	Weekday ヨウ you

Compounds:
曜日
ようび youbi
day of week

日曜日
にちようび
nichiyoubi
sunday

火曜日
かようび kayoubi
tuesday

水曜日
すいようび
suiyoubi
wednesday

有	Have, exist ユウ yuu あ(る) aru

Compounds:

有名
ゆうめい yuumei
famous

有る
ある aru
have

有用
ゆうよう yuuyou
useful

KANJI PRACTICE WORKSHEET

服	Clothing フク fuku

Compounds:

服
 ふく fuku
 clothes

洋服
 ようふく youfuku
 western clothes

作業服
 さぎょうふく
 sagyoufuku
 uniform

服	服	服	服	服	服
服	服	服	服	服	服
服	服	服	服	服	服
服	服	服	服	服	服
服	服	服	服	服	服
服	服	服	服	服	服
服	服	服	服	服	服
服	服	服	服	服	服

朝	Morning, period チョウ chou あさ asa

Compounds:

朝
 あさ asa
 morning

毎朝
 まいあさ maiasa
 every morning

朝食
 ちょうしょく
 choushoku
 breakfast

朝	朝	朝	朝	朝	朝
朝	朝	朝	朝	朝	朝
朝	朝	朝	朝	朝	朝
朝	朝	朝	朝	朝	朝
朝	朝	朝	朝	朝	朝
朝	朝	朝	朝	朝	朝
朝	朝	朝	朝	朝	朝
朝	朝	朝	朝	朝	朝

KANJI PRACTICE WORKSHEET

村	Town, village ソン son むら mura

Compounds:

村
　むら mura
　village

山村
　さんそん sanson
　mountain village

村人
　むらびと murabito
　villager

林	Forest リン rin はやし hayashi

Compounds:

林
　はやし hayashi
　woods, forest

森林
　しんりん shinrin
　forest

林業
　りんぎょう ringyou
　forestry

KANJI PRACTICE WORKSHEET

森	Forest, woods シン shin もり mori

Compounds:

森
もり mori
forest

森林
しんりん shinrin
forest

業	Business ギョウ gyou

Compounds:

業者
ぎょうしゃ
gyousha
trader

工業
こうぎょう
kougyou
manufacturing industry

休業
きゅうぎょう
kyuugyou
closed (store)

KANJI PRACTICE WORKSHEET

楽

Music, comfort, easy

ラク raku, ガク gaku
たの(しい)　tano(shii)

Compounds:

楽
らく raku
comfort, ease

音楽
おんがく ongaku
music

楽しい
たのしい tanoshii
enjoyable

歌

Song, sing

カ ka
うた uta

Compounds:

歌
うた uta
song, poetry

歌う
うたう utau
to sing

歌手
かしゅ kashu
singer

KANJI PRACTICE WORKSHEET

止	Stop シ shi と(まる) to(maru)

Compounds:

中止
ちゅうし chuushi
suspension, stoppage

止まる
とまる tomaru
to remain, to stay

休止
きゅうし kyuushi
pause, rest

正	Correct, righteous セイ sei, ショウ shou ただ(しい) tada(shii)

Compounds:

正しい
ただしい tadashii
correct, truthful, righteous

正月
しょうがつ shougatsu
New Year's Day, the first month

正体
しょうたい shoutai
natural shape

KANJI PRACTICE WORKSHEET

歩	Walk ホ ho, ブ bu, フ fu ある(く) aru(ku)

Compounds:

歩く
あるく aruku
to walk

進歩
しんぽ shinpo
to progress, to develop

牛歩
ぎゅうほ gyuuho
snail's pace

死	Death, die シ shi し(ぬ) shi(nu)

Compounds:

死ぬ
しぬ shinu
to die

死人
しにん shinin
corpse, dead person

病死
びょうし byoushi
natural death

KANJI PRACTICE WORKSHEET

民

People, nation

ミン min
たみ tami

Compounds:

民
たみ tami
nation, people

民間
みんかん minkan
private, unofficial, civilian

民族
みんぞく minzoku
people

池

Pond, pool

チ chi
いけ ike

Compounds:

池
いけ ike
pond

電池
でんち denchi
battery

電池切れ
でんしぎれ
denchigire
Low battery

KANJI PRACTICE WORKSHEET

注	Pour, concentrate チュウ chuu そそ(ぐ) soso(gu)

Compounds:

注ぐ
そそぐ sosogu
to pour, to fill

注文
ちゅうもん
chuumon
order, request

注意
ちゅうい chuui
attention

洋	Ocean ヨウ you

Compounds:

海洋
かいよう kaiyou
ocean

洋風
ようふう youfuu
western style

洋食
ようしょく
youshoku
western style meal

KANJI PRACTICE WORKSHEET

洗	Wash セン sen あら(う) ara(u)					
Compounds: 洗う あらう arau to wash 洗濯 せんたく sentaku washing, laundry 洗車 せんしゃ sensha car wash						

海	Sea, ocean カイ kai うみ umi					
Compounds: 海 うみ umi sea, beach 海外 かいがい kaigai overseas, abroad 北海道 ほっかいどう hokkaido						

KANJI PRACTICE WORKSHEET

漢	China カン kan

Compounds:

漢字
かんじ kanji
Chinese character

牛	Cow ギュウ gyuu うし ushi

Compounds:

牛
うし ushi
cow

牛肉
ぎゅうにく
gyuuniku
beef

水牛
すいぎゅう suigyuu
water buffalo

KANJI PRACTICE WORKSHEET

物

Thing, object

モツ motsu
ブツ butsu
もの mono

Compounds:

建物
たてもの tatemono
building

買い物
かいもの kaimono
shopping

動物
どうぶつ doubutsu
animal

特

Special

トク toku

Compounds:

特別
とくべつ tokubetsu
special

特に
とくに tokuni
particularly,
especially

特集
とくしゅう
tokushuu
special feature

KANJI PRACTICE WORKSHEET

犬	Dog ケン ken いぬ inu

Compounds:

犬
いぬ inu
Dog

理	Logic, reason リ ri

Compounds:

理
り ri
reason

料理
りょうり ryouri
cooking, cuisine

物理
ぶつり butsuri
physics

KANJI PRACTICE WORKSHEET

産	Product, give birth サン san う (む) u(mu)

Compounds:

産業
さんぎょう
sangyou
industry

不動産
ふどうさん
fudousan
real estate

産む
うむ umu
to give birth

用	Use, utilize ヨウ you もち(いる) mochi(iru)

Compounds:

用
よう you
task, business, use

信用
しんよう shinyou
confidence

起用
きよう kiyou
appointment

KANJI PRACTICE WORKSHEET

田	Rice field デン den た ta

Compounds:

田
た ta
rice field

町	Town, village チョウ chou まち machi

Compounds:

町
まち machi
town, street

町中
まちなか
machinaka
downtown

KANJI PRACTICE WORKSHEET

画

Picture

ガ ga
カク kaku

Compounds:

映画
えいが eiga
movie, film

計画
けいかく keikaku
plan, schedule

画家
がか gaka
painter, artist

界

World

カイ kai

Compounds:

世界
せかい sekai
world

学界
がっかい gakkai
academic world

外界
がいかい gaikai
physical world

KANJI PRACTICE WORKSHEET

| 病 | Ill, sick |
| | ビョウ byou |

Compounds:

病院
びょういん byouin
hospital

病気
びょうき byouki
sick

病人
びょうにん
byounin
sick person

| 発 | Departure, disclose |
| | ハツ hatsu |

Compounds:

発言
はつげん hatsugen
proposal, speech

出発
しゅっぱつ
shuppatsu
departure

発見
はっけん hakken
discovery

KANJI PRACTICE WORKSHEET

県	Prefecture ケン ken

Compounds:

県
けん ken
prefecture

県内
けんない kennai
within the prefecture

真	True, reality シン shin

Compounds:

写真
しゃしん shashin
photograph

真中
まんなか mannaka
centre, mid-way

真理
しんり shinri
truth

KANJI PRACTICE WORKSHEET

着	Arrive, wear チャク　　chaku き（る）ki(ru), つ（く）tsu(ku)

Compounds:

着る
きる kiru
to wear

着く
つく tsuku
to arrive

着物
きもの
kimono

知	Know チ chi し（る）shi(ru)

Compounds:

知る
しる shiru
to know

知らせ
しらせ shirase
notice

人見知り
ひとみしり
hitomishiri
shyness

KANJI PRACTICE WORKSHEET

短	Short, defect タン tan みじか (い) mijika(i)

Compounds:

短い
みじかい mijikai
short

短気
たんき tanki
short temper

研	Polish, sharpen, study ケン ken と (ぐ) to(gu)

Compounds:

研究
けんきゅう
kenkyuu
research

研究者
けんきゅうしゃ
kenkyuusha
researcher

研修
けんしゅう
kenshuu
training

KANJI PRACTICE WORKSHEET

私	I, me シ shi わたし watashi

Compounds:

私
 わたし watashi
 Me, I

私学
 しがく shigaku
 private school

私服
 しふく shifuku
 plain clothes

秋	Autumn あき aki

Compounds:

秋
 あき aki
 autumn

秋風
 あきかぜ akikaze
 autumn breeze

KANJI PRACTICE WORKSHEET

究	Research, study キュウ kyuu きわ(める) kiwa(meru)

Compounds:

研究
けんきゅう
kenkyuu
research, study

学究
がっきゅう
gakkyuu
scholar

研究員
けんきゅういん
kenkyuuin
researcher

答	solution, answer トウ tou こた(え) kota(e)

Compounds:

答え
こたえ kotae
answer

問答
もんどう mondou
questions and
answers

KANJI PRACTICE WORKSHEET

紙	Paper シ shi かみ kami

Compounds:

紙
　かみ kami
　paper

手紙
　てがみ tegami
　letter

用紙
　ようし youshi
　blank form

終	End, finish シュウ shuu お(わる) o(waru)

Compounds:

終わる
　おわる owaru
　to finish, to close

終わり
　おわり owari
　the end

KANJI PRACTICE WORKSHEET

習	Learn シュウ shuu なら(う) nara(u)						
Compounds: 習う ならう narau to learn 教習 きょうしゅう kyoushuu training, instruction 見習う みならう minarau to follow one's example							

考	Consider, think over コウ kou かんが(える) kanga(eru)						
Compounds: 考える かんがえる kangaeru to think, to consider 考え かんがえ kangae thought, idea 考え方 かんがえかた kangaekata way of thinking							

KANJI PRACTICE WORKSHEET

者	Someone, person シャ sha もの mono

Compounds:

者
もの mono
person

業者
ぎょうしゃ
gyousha
trader, merchant

死者
ししゃ shisha
deceased

肉	Meat ニク niku

Compounds:

肉
にく niku
meat

牛肉
ぎゅうにく
gyuuniku
beef

肉屋
にくや nikuya
butcher

KANJI PRACTICE WORKSHEET

自	Oneself ジ ji みずか（ら）mizuka(ra)					
Compounds: 自分 じぶん jibun oneself 自動 じどう jidou automatic 自転車 じてんしゃ jitensha bicycle						

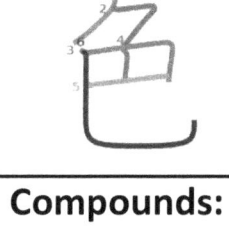

	Colour シキ shiki, ショク shoku いろ iro					
Compounds: 色 いろ iro colour 黄色 きいろ kiiro yellow 色々 いろいろ iroiro various						

KANJI PRACTICE WORKSHEET

英	England, English エイ ei

Compounds:

英語
えいご eigo
the English language

英文
えいぶん eibun
sentence in English

英明
えいめい eimei
intelligent

茶	Tea サ sa チャ cha

Compounds:

お茶
おちゃ ocha
(green) tea

茶色
ちゃいろ chairo
brown

茶道
さどう sadou
Tea Ceremony

KANJI PRACTICE WORKSHEET

菜

Vegetable, greens

な na
サイ sai

Compounds:

野菜
やさい yasai
vegetables

白菜
はくさい hakusai
Chinese cabbage,
white rape

菜食
さいしょく
saishoku
vegetable diet

薬

Medicine

ヤク yaku
くすり　　　kusuri

Compounds:

薬
くすり kusuri
medicine,
pharmaceuticals

火薬
かやく kayaku
gun powder

薬学
やくがく yakugaku
study of pharmacy

KANJI PRACTICE WORKSHEET

親

Parent, relative

シン shin
おや oya
した(しい)　shita(shii)

Compounds:

親
おや oya
parents

両親
りょうしん
ryoushin
parents

親切
しんせつ shinsetsu
kindness

計

Plot, plan, measure

ケイ kei
はか(る)　haka(ru)

Compounds:

計画
けいかく keikaku
plan, project, program

時計
とけい tokei
watch, clock

計る
はかる hakaru
to measure

KANJI PRACTICE WORKSHEET

試	Test, try シ shi ため(す) tame(su)					
Compounds: 試合 　しあい shiai 　match 試験 　しけん shiken 　exam, test 試食 　ししょく shishoku 　sampling food						

説	Opinion, theory セツ setsu と(く) to(ku)					
Compounds: 説明 　せつめい setsumei 　explanation 小説 　しょうせつ shousetsu 　novel, short story 説 　せつ setsu 　theory						

KANJI PRACTICE WORKSHEET

貸	Lend タイ tai か (す) ka(su)
Compounds: 貸す かす kasu to lend 貸し かし kashi loan	(practice grid)

質	Quality, matter シツ shitsu
Compounds: 質 しつ shitsu quality 質問 しつもん shitsumon question, inquiry 水質 すいしつ suishitsu water quality	(practice grid)

KANJI PRACTICE WORKSHEET

赤	Red セキ seki, シャク　　shaku あか aka
Compounds: 赤い 　あかい akai 　red 赤ちゃん 　あかちゃん akachan baby	(practice grid)

走	Run ソウ sou はし(る)　hashi(ru)
Compounds: 走る 　はしる hashiru 　to run 走り書き 　はしりがき hashirigaki scribble	(practice grid)

KANJI PRACTICE WORKSHEET

起	Wake, get up キ ki お(きる) o(kiru) お(こる) o(koru)

Compounds:

起きる
おきる okiru
to wake up

起こる
おこる okoru
to occur, to happen

転	Revolve, turn around テン ten ころ(ぶ) koro(bu)

Compounds:

転じる
てんじる tenjiru
to turn, to shift

自転車
じてんしゃ
jitensha
bicycle

回転
かいてん kaiten
roll

KANJI PRACTICE WORKSHEET

軽	Light ケイ kei かる(い) karu(i)

Compounds:

軽い
かるい karui
light, non-serious

軽口
かるくち karuguchi
talkative, loose-lipped

軽音楽
けいおんがく
keiongaku
light music

近	Near キン kin ちか(い) chika(i)

Compounds:

近い
ちかい chikai
near, close by

近所
きんじょ kinjo
neighbourhood

付近
ふきん fukin
vicinity

KANJI PRACTICE WORKSHEET

送	Send ソウ sou おく(る) oku(ru)

Compounds:

送る
おくる okuru
to send, to see off (person)

送別
そうべつ soubetsu
farewell

送電
そうでん souden
electric supply

通	Pass through, commute ツウ tsuu かよ(う) kayo(u)

Compounds:

通う
かよう kayou
to commute

通信社
つうしんしゃ tsuushinsha
newsagency

貫通
かんつう kantsuu
Pass through

KANJI PRACTICE WORKSHEET

進	Advance, proceed シン shin すす(む) susu(mu)

Compounds:

進む
 すすむ susumu
 to make progress

進歩
 しんぽ shinpo
 progress

進捗
 しんちょく
 shinchoku
 progress

運	Transport, progress ウン un はこ(ぶ) hako(bu)

Compounds:

運ぶ
 はこぶ hakobu
 to transport

運動
 うんどう undou
 exercise

運転
 うんてん unten
 driving, motion

遠

Distant, far

エン en, オン on
とお(い) too(i)

Compounds:

遠い
とおい tooi
far, distant

遠足
えんそく ensoku
trip, hike, picnic

遠心力
えんしんりょく
enshinryoku
centrifugal force

都

Metropolis, capital

ト to, ツ tsu
みやこ miyako

Compounds:

都
みやこ miyako
capital

京都
きょうと kyouto
Kyoto (city)

都会
とかい tokai
city

Conclusion

Mastering these 168 essential kanji will greatly improve your ability to read and understand Japanese at the N4 level. While learning kanji can seem challenging at first, consistent practice and exposure will make it easier over time.

Remember to reinforce your learning by reading real Japanese texts, writing kanji by hand, and using them in context. These characters will serve as a strong foundation, helping you progress toward more advanced levels of Japanese.

Keep practicing, stay patient, and enjoy the journey of learning kanji. Ganbatte!

www.ingramcontent.com/pod-product-compliance
Lightning Source LLC
LaVergne TN
LVHW070221080526
838202LV00068B/6875